Freak Show

Casey Killingsworth

Fernwood
PRESS

Freak Show

Fernwood Press
Newberg, Oregon
www.fernwoodpress.com

Printed in the United States of America

Cover and page design: Mareesa Fawver Moss
Author photo: Eva Reese

ISBN 978-1-59498-130-2

To F.A. Nettelbeck, who came to be a real poet when he drove to Beatty, Oregon, and never left.

Contents

Foreword

I am a professional guitarist living in the Willamette Valley of Oregon. I have performed in night clubs and festivals throughout the Pacific Northwest for the past forty years. My career has been built on my love and passion for Blues and R&B music culminating in numerous Blues awards and recognition from the Cascade Blues Association in Portland.

In May of 1980, I started a job stocking groceries on a freight crew where I met Casey. There was an instant connection between us. Casey, himself a talented singer/songwriter, provided the perfect path and bond that have lasted these last four decades. We also shared a great sense of humor that made those long hard nights tolerable.

It's been said that people come in and out of our lives; some stay for a short time and others for a lifetime. The latter has certainly been the case for Casey and me. And now he has asked me to write something to introduce his new book of poems, *Freak Show.* And I'm happy to do it, happy to let you know that in life you can be both a poet or a musician and a graveyard stock clerk, because Casey and I have worn all those hats. I remember sitting around on our breaks in the middle of the night talking about what we would do if we ever got unshackled from that graveyard shift.

First let me say that you should be careful reading these poems, particularly the ones about the life of a laborer. While they often address loss or missing out on something, this is not a collection that lacks hope. It's rather a lens for hard living, for loss with resilience, for the case of continuing to try even in the face of that loss. So in the end, the harshness of the laborer's life still manages to sound like optimism.

To a certain degree that world is a different world, one that few people who don't experience it see. That's partly what's important about these poems. In those pieces, Casey is revealing that existence, what it's like to go to work in the middle of the night and do your job sequestered from the rest of the world. You should listen to him, listen to what that world is like:

> . . . working while you slept,
> trying to be quiet so I didn't wake you, missing the sun.
> Every time you woke to pee or get a glass of water
> I was watering a golf course or sending trucks
> out from some post office dock, and on
> your way to work I was on my first beer.

Still, it would be too simple to think this collection is only about working in the blue-collar world or about working oddball shifts because Casey also digs into the universal emotions none of us can escape, like, for instance, grief or alienation. So when there's a duck—yes, a duck—wandering around the center of town, Casey captures the inescapable sense of feeling alone, even when you're in the middle of town, even when you're a duck:

> Still, when you see that duck you
> have to pick it up and walk it clear down
> to Rock Cove and set it down with the
> other ducks and watch it fly straight out
> over the river, as if there were some list
> in the world, as if there were some order
> and the duck is merely playing out its part.

But of course there is no order so you
pick up the duck just because it's a duck
on the sidewalk in the middle of town,
because you have to, because you
can't go back home empty-handed
without helping the world out
just a little.

Or so it seems to me.

Really, I guess, this book is about trajectories, about what happens when our lives spin in directions we didn't see coming and point us down paths that we find out only later are either good or bad. Casey and I have had our share of these directional shifts, and now as we both get old, we get to do pretty much what we want, me playing guitar, Casey writing poems, without worrying about other work anymore. So in the end, we both got to live right next to that good path after all.

Or so it seems to me.

Garry Meziere
April 2022

Freak show

My sister has had a hell of a time with life.
My mother said even when we were kids
she would catalog all the toys in her room
into paper bags—no playing, just organizing—
for what reason nobody knows.

When she got older the boys in the mall would
turn and stare, not realizing that this beauty
had a history with paper bags, that she was
odd in a way that given a choice they would
cash their dreams of her in at the food court.

My sister worked hard in a grocery store bakery
where one night on the walk home she got raped,
by which I mean she became even more organized
and lived a life where there were never enough
ice cubes, or jar lids, or drawers to store her world in.

I have never questioned the idea of a bearded lady
in some traveling show, but I am guilty of wondering why
she wouldn't just shave it off. Maybe she liked the attention,
or maybe they paid her well, or maybe in the mirror
we just don't notice who we become, who we are.

Or maybe we just glance and accept it, no matter what.
But even if the strong man's weights are lighter than air, or
if sword swallowing is simply an illusion, still our fascination
never speaks to the idea of forgiveness, and my sister is still
waiting backstage for us to pay our admission to watch her fall.

A nest blew down

It's not like losing a child
where you just sit there
and the child just sits there
but you're the only one
doing the talking.
It's more like a placenta
out of sticks and mud
in the driveway,
a former home where
something was born
and left, or maybe was
born and never got to
leave or was swept
away by the wind
that came through
here last night, maybe
more like having a house
burn to the ground,
no big deal if you have
wings to take you
somewhere else.

Reprise

Yesterday something delivered a short vision of what I thought
the world was like thirty years ago; it hit me like that pain
in your side the doctor said was nothing.

For two days now there's been a fisherman in the middle
of the river, standing like an island there on such a day like today
with all the rain and sad skies.

I wouldn't think there would be any fish in the river right now
anyway but there he is, aiming his pole precisely toward a hole
in the water as if there were a guaranteed return

if only he could hit that hole. I used to like fishing myself,
not that I ever did it, but I liked watching the geometry of the line
just before it hit the water,

waiting for the dumb fish to commit to swallowing the fake
thrashing bug. I used to think fishing must be something good,
a place you could bring your kids, a memory

you could casually fold in your pocket and discover years later
when you pull that old pair of pants out of the closet and stuff
your hands inside searching for forgotten prizes.

Now it's just one more hollow challenge, something you do
because you told yourself you would, you'd get up this morning,
you'd get up and wade knee-deep in some river,

no matter what.

199 words for 29 people who were not on the Edmund Fitzgerald

The day the big ship went down a boy died while
on vacation. He was asleep in the back of his
parents' pickup camper when a rock with his name
on it rolled down the mountain and killed him.

Except for his parents, who probably died years
ago, probably of grief, I'm the only one who thinks
about how a rock could have anybody's name on it.
And why. And why he hasn't been counted over time.

And how do you count the dead anyway; are they
one or zero, the ones who don't make it into songs,
the ones who never make it onto milk cartons,
are they only placeholders until a new baby is born
and the kid in the truck becomes just a remainder?

But this isn't about that kid or his rock; it's about
numbers, about quantities, about who gets counted
in the world and how history is made in boardrooms
and music studios but not factories, because

maybe when we live there is a part that's bigger than
who gets to own a shiny legacy; it has to do with
the dreams that kid never dreamed, it has to do
with looking for a rock with your name on it.

Two friends in Bend

For whatever reason my two childhood
friends ended up in Bend, a place

I have never lived. One just retired
from being some bigshot in some

big company and the other is there
because that's where they place people

who no longer remember their own names.
Sometimes I go and visit them,

the one to remember the old times,
and the other to remember the old times.

Circus

I saw on a television show once
that in the circus everyone has
two jobs. One is the glory job,
flying on the trapeze, knife
throwing, that sort of thing.
The other is the shirtsleeve job,
the everyday work, the cleaning up
elephant shit, the whatever.
The circus can't run unless
everyone does two jobs.

In my dreams my glory job is
to drive the train, the circus train,
pulling animals and clowns
around the world to smiling kids.
When I worked on the railroad all
we wanted was to be train drivers
instead of ground pukes
pushing ties under a thousand pound rail,
all to keep some soft engineer riding
high on the way to some exotic place.

In my dreams my shirtsleeve job would
not be to stack cans on shelves all night in
a grocery store, would not be to
get held up at knifepoint one night
after the store is closed and we're locked in
waiting for the day shift losers to let us out,
would not be to let a car run me over
on my bike my second night of work,
but still work my shift because
I'm too scared I'll get fired if I don't.

I would rather shovel elephant shit
than work in a grocery store
all night. But we all have to have two jobs,
we all have to live between the glory job
twirling on that trapeze, and
our shirtsleeve job, where safety
nets stretch every direction but never
stretch far enough to break our fall.

What a dream is

Don't try writing a poem on
the graveyard shift, don't try

to vote on the Senate floor if
you've ever borrowed money

for rent from the guy next door
whose name you do not know,

don't wear a tie with blisters
on your hands and don't try

to pronounce elegant drink names
when there are lawyers

two barstools down, just don't.

Application for acceptance into humanity

One night some old worker might
yell across the pub, "Hey Blondie,
is that you?" Nobody's called me
that in like forever but I yell back yeah

it's me and somehow recognize
the guy through layers of years
ago on the railroad; God he's a relic,
he's been beaten into the ground

under that desert sun for years after
I left, looks like, and he says loud
enough for Bob and everyone to hear,
"This guy here, he worked hard,

so hard, harder than the rest of us,
strong, strong as a horse who doesn't
have better sense than to apply for a job
pounding spikes into the world all day."

And the evening goes on the same
after that, maybe illuminated just
a little under the thinnest lightness
of glory.

Nature/commerce

The fish in Rock Creek are UPS trucks
lined up to load out at the docks,

the blue jays are the teletype machines
from 1950s stock market movies,

the waving grass in the field down from
our house is the ocean on a warm day—

no—the piston driving any GMC engine,
and the dark and still of last night

are the union breaks we get so we can
go back out there and be more productive.

And now, the one, the only, Casey the Brave

The last time I was scared, besides the night in the back of
the grocery store with knives, was when they wouldn't
let me back into the movie theater after I ran out,

the big screen too small to hold my little kid fears and
no place to go because my parents drove off,
trusting me to act like a big boy.

You don't scare me. I was around when we fought wars
against capital letter doctrines, before computers,
and don't get me started about assassinations.

Okay, maybe I was afraid of new songs, people I didn't know,
drinks I couldn't pronounce. The thing is, I'm not a big boy.
Fear gets bought out by anger, anger by numbness,
and numbness is just a scaredy cat

without claws.

The history of the world for as long as I can remember

As far as I know there really is some pattern to the
billions of poems we have left behind, you know,
the old applications for jobs we never got, clandestine
napkin messages to waitresses in the bars we drank at,
the arguments we had with our wives that ended up as
divorce documents, all those scraps of paper still orbiting
the world like greenhouse gasses.

At least that's the way I see it.

Sometimes I like to believe all those scraps, the
slices of memoirs we sacrificed for a single moment's
clear image of the universe, they're like those little birds
always flying synchronously together like storm clouds
in the wind, an arc or maybe not an arc but all moving in
the same direction, because all we can do is look up
to try to figure out what they mean. But we can't.

So how about this: what if all of history is contained in
some woman you barely know, say an older woman, say
one who checks your groceries out at the local market,
who worked at Subway every Saturday of her life but caught
a break when she got hired at the store and then got
promoted to manager—which you didn't know because,

you know, you're busy too—which really helped because her
partner of twenty-eight years died and she had to make it on her own,
what if all of history was defined in terms of her, everything that
ever was, and is, poured into a vessel the size of the person scanning
your cereal, hanging onto her every rotation around the earth?
What if?

Car salesman

My father's story about his father's unfulfilled
salesman life always came glued to the back
of a story about my grandmother dying
when he was still such a young boy.

My grandfather drank too much, sure, was always
moving to the next shitty L.A. apartment above
the next sketchy drug store, and he drove
through traffic like Neal Cassady, so there is that.

His trajectory lives in me through some wireless
intravenous cord, but unfulfilled is not what this is.
That word is just cheap medicine patching a gash
in the stratosphere with a piece of duct tape.

It's biology, it's the rushing of some genetic caffeine
that keeps pushing me someplace not good, it's the
chosen path a river takes when it's new, that's all.
Besides, that old man never said a mean word

to anyone, always had a ten-year-old's wonder
of the world that swirled around him, and kept
a vigil over us by never sleeping, watching and
worrying about the news until the TV signed off.

Once I surprised him in his apartment after one
of his three-day drunks and he still wanted me to
drive him to some observatory where he pointed
out every detail of the shrill beauty of

a huge telescope big enough to see the past life
of stars, but not big enough to watch a man without
oxygen struggle to catch his breath inside the middle
of a big city.

One night in a Mexican restaurant with your small son, talking about death

It's hard to know what to order, the chicken enchiladas are good,
or maybe something with seafood, both are packed with death,

and finally you have to face it, your son's anxious face waiting for
news of a new sister or brother, looking as earnest as a dessert menu,

and you start with the standard: everything has to die, must
eventually live only in our hearts, blah blah but you're interrupted

when the waitress tells you they're out of margaritas, they're out of
fucking margaritas, and you lose your place in the speech and,

and instead of returning to the script that had died a death already
you move to his side of the booth and just sit there next to him,

you sit and wait, you both wait for somebody to deliver something,
the salsa maybe, or a side of consolation, to your table.

Obituarians dream in happy words

The obituarian works
seven days a week not
because people are dying
but because they could be.
What I mean is he's on call.

The obituarian never takes
a lover because he has no way
to tell the truth; all he knows is
to tell every dead person they
were great and meaningful.
What I mean is he's lonely.

The obituarian has a way
with words. Those words can't
count a life, but they are
the living's only hope in death.
What I mean is he's a poet.

Home run

There is a name for when rich people can't decide
which of their houses to drive to for the holiday while
other people are discovering the nutritional value of
poverty, but I don't know what it is so I'm going to call it
Sometimes you're the baseball, sometimes you're the bat.

When I get to pick the teams, my designated hitter
will be the ball, which most of the time gets
the shit beat out of it, but every once in a while it
sails over the fence and the roar of the crowd erases
the pain as if the bruises weren't even there.

I wonder why we are all like onlookers in a sideshow,
believing that the snake oil will cure us, but we know
it's not true, but we still believe it is. We believe it
like we believe that when it's our turn to bat
the ball will rise up high, high above the cheap seats
and summer homes, and never come back.

Cub scout blows it with Catholic school girl

I'm sorry I didn't buy us tickets
for the dance. I had the money
sitting right there but I didn't know
how to talk to girls. Or dance.

I'm sorry I didn't stay in scouts
after the leader told me I had
to wear my uniform or else. God,
you looked good in your uniform.

I'm sorry I didn't make anything
of my life, sorry I didn't get that
degree, sorry I never memorized
the scout credo.

Except I'm not sorry, not sorry
I quit the scouts, not sorry I can't
spell catechism, not sorry
I had struggles.

I am sorry, though, that
I didn't buy those tickets.

What we can't afford to tell second graders

There's some kid somewhere playing cello,
practicing the same three notes over and over
until his fingers ignite, but they tell him to keep
up his practice, and he does, and, of course,
he becomes very good and famous, etc.

As you might already suspect, this is the dream
we all have the night before we're called upon
to tell our classmates what we will be when
we grow up, signing contracts, touring the big
concert halls, our name announced on printed pages.

But when it's our turn in front of the class we hesitate,
remembering that the cello dream was the dream of
a dream, that our own dream was the one with sad
marriages and night shifts, first and last month's rent,
realization that the number of musicians in the world

is both fixed and secret, and old student cellos leaned up
in the backs of closets.

Silence

> *It is in the thick of calamity that one gets hardened to the truth—in other words, to silence.*
>
> *Albert Camus*

My father lost most of his hearing in a war he still
defends, and the rest he lost to indefensible time.
It's a silent world, one where he talks but can't hear,
one where all we do is listen to him but can't speak,
like his voice is the period at the end of an essay.

All the black-and-white photos of my childhood, the
ones where all of us kids are singing around a country
kitchen table playing our little instruments, my father
is at the periphery of the frame, harboring every word
and hesitant to be part of the picture.

When we visit now he shuffles over to that same table
in his kitchen to get a visual clue to what song we—
my brother and I, old men now ourselves—are singing,
and he starts humming. There are notes in silence, you
know, placeholders for what can never be spoken or heard.

Yes, music has been a part of my life. I hear songs where some
hear only commerce, like some truck pulling away from a
midnight dock singing harmony with the poverty in my bones.
I know my father can't hear these songs, but he reads
the lyrics. And he hums. And sometimes he remembers the words.

The civil war inside me

My mother sorted her beans
in a strainer because you never
know when someone might slip
a rock into the package
you never know and the least
you could lose is a tooth

or maybe the sorting machines
or a tired worker accidentally let one
little rock slip through on the belt
and wham! you're in the dentist
chair. I've never been to church.

I don't understand how it works—
what I mean is I don't know what
church is for and
I don't think you do either—
all that praying and singing to
someone you can't even see.

Only once I prayed, to have all the
rocks end up in someone else's bowl
and my mother said that's not
the way it works but she was there
then and Jesus wasn't and now
someone needs to step up and
show me how to sort these beans.

The half life of moons

You and your wife are fighting again
and just as you step into round three
the world slows down and then speeds up
like a gyre and as you glance inside it
the argument begins to shrivel
and you see your life within
the thin circumference of its years,
and beyond that you see your
young grandparents dancing to some
battle song, and further back
ancient soldiers shooting at the
universal secret fear that the world
was more than they could know,
back through wars fought with knuckles,
entire villages of real people buried
under layers of myths that could explain
anything, and then you see, light years
ahead, ________, indescribable
in our languages, so far advanced
our descendants have found better ways
than war to maim themselves. And yet,
somehow, the world lives on, past you,
past grandparents and soldiers
and all future funerals, and you can't
even remember why you were fighting.
Goddamn it. Goddamn it.
Who are these people screaming?

If I were to define religion

Say there's
an old friend someday
who mentions a name, mine,
or say there's a smell from
some small café or
even the hint of a spring day
like this one
out of the west,
holding off the
rest of winter.

Wherever you are
put down your fork.
Wrap the remaining bread
in a napkin and
walk back
here to this day.
Find it in yourself
to say "pleasant."
Wasn't it? Isn't it?

Why do we say we find peace when we die?

I don't know what the ingredients are for a world
that's unraveling but one might be the sound
an owl makes with your car as it fixes
on a mouse across a highway and you're in
the way,

past headlights and almost past metal bumpers
that scream at it to pull off, to stand down,
to save itself on a dark night
that suddenly becomes darker
after you hear the sound.

And when you realize that something happened,
not your fault, not anyone's fault,
just happened, if it's part of a script
that you were forced to follow by some invisible
dictator's hand, then that's too bad.

And if it's not a script but simply a thing, some thing,
an event that just was, a collision of different worlds
kind of like no-fault insurance for bumper cars,
and without even a story to tell us how to feel,
well then, that's too bad too.

What if your job

I fooled myself for years that all the jobs
I worked were better than one long career
because without a career I had more time
to spend not thinking about work. But really,
like you, I'd rather not work at all. What if
we got paid for nothing, not even for doing
things we love to do, like the singer in a band,
where sure, it's fun but there's still pressure
to perform, but just for living. There would be
no ties between what you get paid and what
you do. You breathe, you get a check.

Once I got paid for how many pounds of beans
I picked. I could pick more beans than most of
the other workers but I wasn't any better, just faster
at picking beans. And anyway, all of us were
there just to get some money; who would pick
beans on an early summer morning if you
didn't have to? We stood in line for the weigher
to weigh our beans like we were waiting to get
picked for a playground team where you have to
wait until the very end just because you can't dribble
the ball, waiting in line to see what we were worth.

Bad luck comes in threes

I wrote something for my daughter, you know,
the one who's not here, because
that's what you're supposed to do. I guess.

Anyway about that same time I got held up
in the back of a store late one night, you know, the
bad-luck-comes-in-threes thing, and it was funny

that after it was all over the other store workers
were more scared than I was, looking over
their shoulders worrying about

whatever they couldn't see. The thing is
those workers never even saw the bad guys,
so maybe what scares us the most is

the unknown, even more than knife blades coming
for our skin, even more than trying to find out
where a daughter, who you had so looked forward to,

where did she go. To ease my pain someone
told me that the moment coming up, the one
that can still go either way, is the moment that counts.

What I'm trying to say here is my third piece
of bad luck was figuring out that waiting for
the next moment is supposed to be a good thing,

not whatever is really coming next,
but the uncertainty of it, you know,
because maybe it could have been some good luck.

At the acupuncturist's

At the acupuncturist's I mention
something about my age and then
realize how silly that sounds, how I could
be that old, could be sixteen high school
careers, older than three people turning
the legal drinking age. It sounds like a joke
from the waiting room, like some twenty-five-year-old
is trying to be funny by referring
to himself as an old man.

Some flightless dove followed me
around the yard yesterday. He had no place
left to go, because where can a dove go who
can't use the sky anymore? So I fed him
and for a second thought about what results
a rescue might bring for a pet dove, for instance,
if there might be acupuncture for birds

or something, but to retrieve him
might be more unbalanced than the cat
we both knew was waiting in the weeds.
I told myself this, that maybe the dove recognized
the objective nature of the world of death
more than I did and maybe he was okay with it all.

But right now I wish I knew an old legend,
from some culture I can't even pronounce,
that tells something about the dove turning
into a hawk, with new wings, and I wish it said
something about me telling a joke about my age,
or maybe even just a little hope to entertain us as
we're waiting for the acupuncturist,
waiting for the cat.

A handbook for water

If you want to know something about me
be prepared to ask this. Ask me this:
ask me about water.

If you want to know something about water
go find that place where Coyote Creek
bubbles up from some spring under King Mountain.
Find where it ran past me as a kid
through the pool that held my skipping stones
through the middle of my romping fields,
through the middle of my years.

Follow where it begins to call
itself the Rogue River
where it pushes and relents
and stumbles and cries against the rocks
until it is finally called this ocean,
where I am.
If you find that then, then
you will know something about water.

1963

1963 was my sister's last best year.
In California she watched cartoons
on Saturday mornings; after the move to Oregon
she made mud pies on the back porch
and watched them dry and crack in
the heat of the summer. She half-washed
carrots from our garden in the creek
that ran by our house and ate them
on the footbridge. It was a good year.

Later, much later, my father said
it was the right thing to do, placing her
"in the loony bin." And now I see it too.
Looking back, she came out of there shining,
looking forward to having two kids and
a good husband, the move to Illinois;
even the difficulty in her joints
that would eventually plague her she gladly
anticipated when they finally let her out.

What happened in between was she
became an artist, not the kind who paints
or even writes, but the kind who sees
the world for what it really is,
like a scientist sees it. My sister,
the artist, had to learn to look away.
She had to learn to pretend the
only things in the world are those
you can count or put in a notebook.
And now, of course, she's fine.
I'd like to tell you this:
if it gets tough watching the
evening news, look out.

The first

The first day on the railroad I learned unlucky is just another word for laborer.

The first time I had sex was nine months before my son was born.

The first time I got divorced I figured out the things you can't believe could happen to you happen to you.

The first time I lost a child I already had the grief stored away.

The first sound I remember hearing was my mother's voice breathing a prayer for my wonderful life.

Almost

I remember the
contestants in the princess
pageants at school
and the heavier
and the stringy-haired
girls in their back row
smiling over the crowd but
really dreaming about almost-
boyfriends until it hurt
in their sleep, young
women whose beautiful
round faces had been
stripped to only a phrase
that whispered they would not,
ever, be chosen, understanding
what the audience pretended
not to know until the
envelope was opened.

And even now, still

For my other daughter

Sometimes I walk past your room and hear you, child,
breathing songs again. I can see me tearing back the covers
to find you still waiting to go outside and play.
The salmon have returned, is what I'm telling you today.
Already they are throwing their scarred bodies
onto the banks of Bear River.

Remember, too, from the bridge we watched a man tag
the eager unknowing fish on their way down the river?
Some will show up in Japan and then swim back here
to this exact spot, he said.
Remember, I dream-whispered to you, *to die.*

You still wriggle and squirm your way into my nights
across a bed of rocks too shallow to find your way home.
Yet I hear you by the dresser, voice softened by time,
and the coolness from the open window is
your swaddling, so long unwrapped.

Why do you tag them, I hear you asking him.
So we can understand where they've been, he says.
I don't know about you, but I don't understand.
I don't understand. I don't understand
why you can't be underneath all those covers.

Comanche

The yacht *Comanche* shattered the world record
for sailing across an ocean, but
when the crew was interviewed
they all said the same thing:
they said the vastness of the sea
is what you think about when you're sailing fast
like that, not the urgency to get the slicing hull
moving toward its finest point, not even
the zeal to win or the close encounters with death,
but the unfathomable and sheer size
of the water that surrounds you. Let's be honest:
it's easy to recognize space in the middle of an ocean.

Everyday I go to work in heavy traffic. I drive under tall
buildings that bend to hide the length of sky that could
help me chart a course. From my view you can't see
the universe or even the expanse of an ocean; from my view
you only stare at tall buildings and listen to the talk about weather,
as if the guy from the corner office could know about
the vicissitudes of a wind or the way continents bow to let sailboats through.
Everyday I drive home from work,
still without knowing anything about the curve of this world,
about where storms come from, or for that matter if there's any way
a boat can really outrun the wind.

I do have hope for the world

This guy in front of me in the drive-thru
has his speakers on "stun" inside his
smoky car that he painted "piece of shit"

on the trunk, with stacks of lumber
barely strapped on top of the dents and
a jungle full of extension cords and tools

heaped in the back seat. I'm thinking he's doing
what he has to, whatever it takes to make
his way in this tough world, and maybe tonight he

just said fuck it, *I'm going to Taco Bell and spending*
every cent I made today and after that I'll go home and
figure out how hard tomorrow is going to kick me.

3:38 a.m.

I work all night throwing tin cans on these
grocery shelves but I dream of working

produce, the light nature of the fruit,
a day job, a benign subject nobody

could ever argue against, and I wonder
if the produce workers embrace each grape

like a single moment or if they only
consider the entire cluster like it was

an hour, or a day, or a year for that matter,
and I wonder if when they sweep the floor

during those daylight hours, on the hour,
every hour, if they mourn the casualties,

the grapes that slip off, lying there useless
on the floor, immediately reduced from

revered badge carelessly dangled by the gods
in all those paintings to only a slipping hazard,

just a weapon trying to take out
all the old ladies squeezing the avocados.

Muzak

Someday you and I might meet in an elevator.
I might nod or move away from my feet, perhaps
look down or ask what floor; who knows?
You might be lonely but instead I might think you're
an exec for a car company; maybe it's the shoes.
You might believe I'm an artist of some kind,
while really I am only visiting my brother on the fortieth floor
or maybe nothing enters your mind or maybe you
wonder how tall I am with only socks on.

Look, this is not some sort of personal ad solicitation;
I don't even know you, okay? It's about the perpetual
negotiation between pack animal and solitary animal,
between reticence and something spoken, anything spoken,
between understanding—okay, there is no understanding—
between the recognition of irrepressible loneliness and yet
wanton dissatisfaction with all the other choices.

Of all the things we might or might not have in common
on that day, this is for sure: we both will not hear the music,
we both will not remember the other riders,
we will both exit on our respective platforms
and let the remaining events of the day wash away
the elevator ride like the writing on one of those toys
we used to draw on when we were both kids, turning it
upside down and shaking it until it is once again blank.
And we will never know if any of this matters.

To the next dove that comes around here

What I missed was the science of the
angle the goshawk took to overcome
the dove in mid-flight, the critical
trajectory we sometimes mistake
for instinct, as if killing something
were in our blood, as if the vanquished
live under a cloud of destiny.

It must be instead something more
like the calculus at Los Alamos,
eight hours a day, five days a week,
year after year, to get all that math
just right, so that when the target
fills up your sight, all you have to do
is dive.

Working on the night shift

When you retire from your work you look
back on the jobs you did as if they were
nothing but stories. When the Easterns
said there is no past, that's what they meant:
other than the pain that's in your bones right
now, the here and now, everything else is just
words you distribute to your younger friends.

Anyway, I did the math the other day and
figured out I spent a third of my working
years on the midnight shift, working while
you slept, trying to be quiet so I didn't
wake you, missing the sun. Every time you
woke to pee or get a glass of water I was
watering a golf course or sending trucks
out from some post office dock, and on
your way to work I was on my first beer.

I did the math and figured out I'm not
tired anymore, at least not the tired that
comes from fighting for the chance to
dream, or from envying sleep like it's my
neighbor's big house. I can go to sleep
whenever I want now, and sometimes
I just want to sleep forever.

Beads for Manhattan

They call it *mitigated land*,
a half-assed attempt to give
back what was taken away,
gaining a square of wetland,
losing to the mall and its people

like the beads for Manhattan
or whatever, as if the hole
they dug is a lake,
as if those shrubs will ever
become a forest,

as if the birds
that might return
here could hold back
their laughter
or tears.

The Lodge

The workers at The Lodge
treat me like a guest when
they see me running
around the golf course.

I wonder how they
would react if they knew
I just sneak in to run
the trails, or worse

I'm just a worker like them.
I want to tell them
hey I work graveyard
and my boss is a piece of shit too,

but sometimes I like
being treated like I'm
a gold club member or maybe
I'm just tired of the looks

I get because of my car
or maybe just tired of how no
money defines me. I tell my
wife poor people don't envy

rich people; they just
want their Porsches. The Lodge
workers never get called
by their last names and the jobs

they do don't have last names
and we say we're sick of them
not smiling when they greet
us at the big fat front door.

Words inside a telephone

My daughter got sacked, again, because the other secretary
in her office misplaced a file and she got blamed. Or something.
I've stopped listening. I don't hear the reasons anymore;
I hear the sounds between each word of the telephone call

that tell me it will be a long while before she's on her own.
What's tough is I come from a line of hard workers,
accepting workers, quiet workers, who did their jobs
without questions, or answers, or speculation.

Their hands worked hard, took the jobs that came around,
went home tired. If you give me some work I'll work, faster than
the next guy, come when you call, stay late or go home early
and you'll leave me alone and that will make us both happy.

If you call this a one-way street, then also call it thunder,
which doesn't ask you if it can roll down a gorge; it just follows
the mountains and river that were already there.
My daughter doesn't know this yet, but she will, she'll work it out,

get another job, maybe one she likes better, maybe not, and
someday she will come back to this moment, right here
where I'm writing from, and figure out we were destined
for work, we were made to go to work every day.

Geography

I don't know where
Bucharest is on the map.
If one of those reporters
on the street asked me,
I would be the poster boy of
ignorance, I would be
why we're going to hell,
why education isn't working.
I am what is wrong with
your world today. I also
couldn't find Pasadena
or Ames, Iowa. Sorry.

In my defense, I can point
to hunger anyplace on any
globe while it's spinning, and
it's easy to locate lamentation
in any town you've ever heard of,
the capital of suffering is regret,
and the pain of poverty is
two million square miles in
area and the main export of
the world is indifference.

Anatomous

If you should rebuild me can you fill me up
out of a river and replace this slow blood
wandering around lost inside of me,
maybe looking for a heart,

install roll-down windows instead of eyes
that will watch instead of observe, squint
instead of judge and let in just a little
of that cool breeze I never see anyway

and maybe you have something to replace these
old hired hands I tried to give up to the bosses,
just like they tell you, sacrifice your hands
but keep the soul, but they wanted all my parts

and speaking of souls, have we decided if
they exist? I was going to ask for one
of those too, but it doesn't seem to go that
well with the world I've been wearing lately.

Love letters from prison

I worked for the post office and
we got stacks of envelopes
from the prison, letters from inmates
to their lovers with lots of artwork
in every address, every letter of the
lover's name exploding with whispery
feathers blowing up each pencil line,
and insecure cherubs announcing the
lover's name, a cry to please open me.

Is there a word less accurate than "inmate"?
The "in" suggests inclusion; "mate," well,
you know. The envelopes were art
and I could barely imagine what beautiful
messages had to be contained inside
based on how much time and work
the inmate had spent
just on that address.
What must these lonely
women have thought just before
they opened their mail?

Here were lovers
loving from behind walls,
forgotten by everyone,
and yet these same exiles writing
with the most desperate,
passionate lover's urgency, with
each word supremely selected
after what,
a month of deliberation?

Helping a lady in her wheelchair to the county building

She asks if I'm embarrassed to be seen pushing her.
When she gets tired and we stop we happen to be on the bridge and

I tell her to look at all the fish down there but she can't because of
her diabetes, can't see them even though they're so thick there's
barely room for water.

She tells me, hon, you're a pretty good guy but after she says people
in the world aren't very nice anymore she upgrades me to really nice.

We stop at the mini mart to buy two diet Mountain Dews because
they're on sale if you buy two and because,
you know, no sugar.

The receptionist at the county barely looks up like I'm only one more
in a long line of samaritans looking for someone else to save.

And I say see you later, and she says next time I'll throw a couple
of bucks your way and I walk on home past the fish
still swimming upstream.

Thick as thieves

I wake up one morning
and there's no car in the
driveway but I'm not going to
call this theft; it's retribution,
paying me back for
my ancestry or maybe
for the time I stole
change from my father's
dresser or when I watched
the grocery checker accidentally
bag a free avocado and I
didn't say anything and I
took it home until it
burned a hole in my
counter and I had to
throw it away from guilt.

We are all thieves. We steal
air from each other,
compete for blades of
grass when we can't even
count all the ones we have,
burn our mouths on
free-trade coffee
and call it suffering
while bums outside wave
at the cold with cold hands
with no coffee, and we tell
our children to hammer
but steal their nails. The
car is gone but I'm not going
to call this theft.
I owe.

Time

There's all this talk about how there is no such thing
as time, or there is, or it's linear, or symmetrical,
whatever. I think of it like a bank account,
how when you're young there never seems to be
enough to pay your bills but really you had enough
all the time and later you think you have more than
you can use, like sometimes you wake up scared
that there won't be enough events to fill up your day.

If you're lucky you can start reinvesting, banking
that time while you're lying there thinking about nothing,
and giving it back to someone, like you're standing
at the intersection next to a guy in some car who's
in a hurry and you wave him through, you wave him
through your right of way, stay an extra few seconds
at the crossroads, maybe even look up at
Red Bluff to see the new way the shadows are
deflecting light off the cliffs this fine morning.

Oranges

This is all I know about oranges.
You hold the frozen can under
a hot tap until you can squeeze
out the concentrated juice and
then add water, like my mother
did every day of my childhood.

Most of the time you forget about
the juicy sweet oranges barely
contained under sun-ripened
skins that come in a box from her
parents, once a year, to remind her
of a warm California childhood.

You watch her eat her orange slowly,
after yours is long gone, and wonder
what memory is she reliving today. You
don't know because she doesn't talk
much about her childhood, but you know
it must have been a good one, the way

she holds on to that orange. You never
hear her complain about moving to
Oregon, where no orange has ever grown,
but she relies upon your father to inform
everyone of how lucky they are to have
escaped that hell-hole, south California.

Hope

The leave-your-message-at-the-beep machine is the
greatest invention ever. When you leave a message you
get a few minutes of hope before the person at the end
of the line calls back and says no to whatever.

These are the moments we collect and keep inside us to
make our lives appear worthwhile, to keep us moving
forward before the disappointment. So, to those I have
left hanging, who have sent me notes unresponded,

who wanted to know how I'm doing, when I was going to
return library books, I've kept quiet for your own good
because hope is the best of all the deadly sins, keeps us
alive just before rejection, the loneliest of sins.

It's what drives us to apply for jobs with no chance of being
accepted because for a while we have a reason to check
the mailbox. Which reminds me, when I drove truck
I heard this story of an old lady who had her frozen food

delivered to her door. When she died they found a garage
full of freezers full of delivered food and figured she
never ate any of it. She just wanted someone to talk to.
So she kept filling her freezers with frozen food,
block after block of frozen hope.

Moon vs. streetlight

In the morning
I watch raccoons
or rather raccoon shadows
moving across the lawn,
the animal itself
somewhere else, probably
still asleep, while the shadow
of it skinks around looking
for food. Before the
imperious sun has time
to chase these shadows
away, I watch lighter
light compete with
itself, watch the
moon, shy as she is,
stretch to overcome a
streetlight, neither
of them strong enough
to turn a shadow into
a raccoon.
I watch the moon
assert herself,
momentarily, and
then defer to the sun
as it comes
from what we
recklessly call
the east, watch her
wither against a brother
too hot and too light
to fight, until I come
back down the stairs
tomorrow morning,
you know, another day.

Grief

I thought you would be taller,
maybe a bit less reclusive.

More embracing, I thought.
You might have also been more

possessive instead of standing
back there at the edge of the

kitchen, beer in hand, nodding
at the conversation but not

really a part of it. I thought
you would shower

your attention upon me, now
that we're in this relationship,

instead of sending cards to others
with those lover's eyes of yours.

Mostly I thought you'd walk
out, the way things always go,

eventually, after I said
something wrong or burned

too many pieces of toast,
maybe stared too long

at my former girlfriend, time.
I thought I'd be alone again.

How God catches us cheating

Our roof mostly works, especially
on sunny days, but we still argue
about the leaks like we're charged
with apportioning a map with
new countries. Do you know
how many buckets you could
fill the attic with for the price
of one roof, I don't say out loud.

The mind is a funny thing.
It punishes the body, gives itself
a time-out for violations like coveting
or eating a grape without
paying for it and it can condemn
its owner like a talk show host.

I don't fight fair. I hang the last roof-
we-didn't-need over her head like a judge
who's not sure what sentence to hand out,
but then hear about it all night whispering
from a voice that sounds like mine
but without the dry rot.

Houses will decay whether or not the
roof leaks, and the rains will end up
inside of what will eventually become
outside, so what are a few drops of water
between friends?

Or so it seems to me

that when you see a duck standing
in front of the bank on your way
to buy beer, it's a sign. Not a sign
like when we pretend there's some
order in the world, or like there's
some list somewhere that compares
every move you make to what
move you should have made,

but a sign that this is not a normal
occurrence. It's not a sign that
it's going to be a bad day or that
you're going to get your beer half-off,
but a sign that the world doesn't
operate according to signs.

Still, when you see that duck you
have to pick it up and walk it clear down
to Rock Cove and set it down with the
other ducks and watch it fly straight out
over the river, as if there were some list
in the world, as if there were some order
and the duck is merely playing out its part.

But of course there is no order so you
pick up the duck just because it's a duck
on the sidewalk in the middle of town,
because you have to, because you
can't go back home empty-handed
without helping the world out
just a little. Or so it seems to me.

Natural selection poem

Every girl I loved
in high school or
at least every one
I dreamed about
ended up with
a boyfriend
from another school
and I hated them
for that because all
the chances I never
had anyway died again,
like running over
a dead animal on
your way home.
I know now they
were instinctively
driven to perpetuate,
to seek out their
best prospects,
the shiny athletes or
intellectual student
body presidents, so
their own babies would
defend the genome,
you know, date boys
from other schools.
I know now it was
just natural selection
because all of us wished
we carried that favored
gene too.

Guitar lessons

My father asks me how often he should change the strings
on his guitar. Wait. Go back. I gave him that guitar,
not a good guitar but good enough, picked it up in a pawn shop
hitchhiking in Canada. Go back some more.

I got off work on a Sunday morning in high school and headed
to California to see my dad's cousin or somebody just because.
When I called my father to tell him what I was doing, all he asked
was if I had my guitar with me.

Back to these days. Once a year, I say, knowing how little
he plays now, change the strings once a year.
And anyhow, he can't even hear his own music anymore--

In the future: he isn't my father just like the guitar is not my guitar.
We claim possession so arbitrarily, like the stones we use to cross
a creek. They're never ours; they just lie in front of us until
we believe the plan was they were meant for our feet all along.

He hands me back the two sets of strings I had given him,
hands me back two years of playing,
hands me back a lifetime of strings for that guitar.

One morning Goodtime Steve sold me drugs in a high school hallway. Sorry, Mom.

When I pulled a pill off this kid,
Steve, for a quarter and sent it
down the toilet, showing—
not just telling—him, the
wickedness of a life like that,
I thought I'd saved his soul,
maybe even the world's soul.
It was my rendering of the
butterfly's wings redirecting
the vast dance of existence.
But I'm not sure it worked.
I never saw Goodtime Steve
after high school. He might
have taken my advice, cleaned
up and become president,
because I don't really keep
track of who the president
is these days, but I suspect
he took my quarter and
bought more drugs and
everything continued as
it would have anyway.
Sometimes when I see
suffering it makes me
wonder what I owe the
world. Is there a list of
our obligations somewhere,
because there have been
times when I could have
used that quarter myself.

President Kennedy

The year we lived in southern California
my dad had the rickety barn in our suburban
backyard torn down. Someone could die, he said.

There were old newspapers with old news
inside that had insulated the barn from
all the years of harsh weather.

Just kidding; in southern California the sun
shines all the time. The insulation was for
something else, I'm not sure what.

The year we lived in southern California the warm
Santa Anas were blowing from the middle of the
ocean right through the hole where that barn had stood.

The winds in Oregon were harder, and struck
like a billboard announcing to new Californians
how cold the rest of the world could be.

The year we lived in southern California
my dad was right: somebody did die.
President Kennedy died. It was a month until

Christmas and the sun watched over the land
like a sheepherder with a borrowed flock, and
I waited on the steps for a new bike as if it were
a good year.

Before names of mountains

There's more action on the river
this morning. Trucks are spilling their
dirt and rocks into the water's edge again,
rolling out a new path or empire, I don't know.

It is already hard to imagine there used to be
a river here, where now new land sits on top of
old water, hard to imagine. But now that I'm
standing here I can sort of feel that water so

recently buried, down through some other land
that was bone dry before the dam, down
to the legend of people who made their lives
under this water, but next to other water.

I can feel their bones and the bones of the fish
that sustained them, through the deeper
parts of stories and dead water that used to be
here, through all legends and before

legends, down before the river, down
before a fledgling creek and someone else's
mountains, down to a holy time
before names of mountains.

Coming to grips with the sound of water

I should live in Tucson
or somewhere parched, with
no water of its own, anyplace
that can only provide me
a few critical drops a day,
just enough to help my lips
form the begging vowel.
(Maybe, also, I should only
breathe in enough air to keep
my lungs apart, not enough
to greed about, so I never
get used to the idea of life.)
I have come upon the sound
of water so often it has become
white noise, an untracked
trickle in the background of my
head. I don't really know about water.

How can I love it like I should
when it is this loud, this available?
Water is objective, it is brash but not
demanding and comes in bottles in
the store, but I just walk past them
on my way to the cheese aisle.
I want to love every drop like a monk
with a grain of rice but when creeks
cross footbridges, when rivers move
bravely in front of me, when oceans
speak words I don't understand,
I treat it as if I'm a customer and
it's the salmon in the window,
on sale this week for $7.99 a pound.

Freeways are stories with white lines

This is a story of the world when I was
young. There is a summer and I am eighteen
or so and I'm riding in an old car on the
freeway with three drunks from Iowa,

or Indiana, but they are carrying
me on this road trip south so I can tell some girl
I knew in high school something. Even then,
riding in that car, playing my banjo in exchange

for the ride, trying to drink beer, I knew what
would remain in the long run, and what would remain
at midnight in San Francisco when they dropped
me off was this story. It would outlast adventure

and shitty work shifts, wives, countless attempts
to finish college, my pledge to save Christmas
cards, what it meant to give a heart, even that
lustful sensation of passing milepost markers
when you're eighteen and hurling south drunk
in an old car toward the whatever will come.

Building a legend out of Lego pieces

My father repeated and added
to his stories so often they now have
lives of their own. Seriously, I think
some of them are naturalized citizens,
immigrating from foreign places like
old letters and often taking a seat
next to me in this kitchen, sometimes
late at night when I'm trying to sort out
other things

like why we so often want to write about
our fathers. My theory now is it's because
we want them to be godperfect—
I know, I know, too much psychology
but give me a second—maybe even god and,
having discovered the fallibility of a
god, we throw it back on the shoulders
of weak, old men we can't forgive.

Tonight it's the story of the Marines versus
Korea, and last night the ascension from the
dirt-floor Arkansas story sat right there
where you're sitting and I laughed out loud
until I cried out loud when he said at my
father's California college they couldn't
understand Southerners when they talked.

Shooting toy bullets at the real war

Recruiters came to my grade school to sign us up as soldiers; okay, that didn't really happen but it sounded like it on the loudspeakers and in the books they made us read. Every mark on the chalkboard was a new strategy for how to win a war.

One thing I didn't read in school was how Al Capone opened a soup kitchen in Chicago during the Depression. They don't teach that kind of myth in school because it's inchoate, doesn't fit for our needs.

In between, when they weren't recruiting me, my brother and I used to play war with toy guns that killed in slow motion, scopes that sensed movement behind the trees long before the enemy could actually see you, long before you would feel the need to protest wars that had yet to be dreamed.

The trophy case

The glass case just outside the gym doors
to me always meant loss, each space between
the trophies a defeat, all the games we didn't win.

I remember
the memorial picture of a girl, mixed in with
the golds and the silvers,

who had an argument with her mother
on the way to school one morning, opened
the car door, and jumped.

I suspect her place in the trophy case was to ease
her parents' pain, to let them know how much
the school understood by locking away their tragedy

inside clear glass with the most cherished of icons,
a dead girl next to the 1963 State Football Champions,
and by locking away the argument,

something so everyday but with the permanence
of an opposing team's winning touchdown,
and when that didn't work how her mother,

dangling in the moment, tried 7,000 ways to fix
that morning, what she might have done differently,
maybe letting her daughter win the argument,

maybe driving another route,
maybe remembering to pick up that loaf of rye bread
on the way.

Taking water away from a river

When your job is watering a golf course
all night you have to find some other
way to make your life worthwhile.

There is this ritual where first thing I walk
to the floating pump house
on the river, feel my way inside

in the dark, and balance just above the water
to clean the pump. I play a game where
every time I lock the door on my way out

I thank someone, really anyone, for not letting
me fall through the opening, for recovering my life,
for not letting the river have me tonight.

If you can envision some patient in a hospital,
a little past panic, who is
preparing to use up her final breath.

And then I flip the power switch
and think about how much control I have of
that river, commanding its water,

sucking it through my pipes underground
to wherever I want it to go and the
river just lies there, helpless as poverty.

If you can envision some five-star despot
screaming at the crowds that he's doing it all for
the country while he's eyeing the farmers' wives.

Even Zeus must get tired of the view sometimes

At some point this place was called
Olympus, home of the gods.

Everything is majestic here, even the brewery
on the other end of town.

Sometimes I forget how lucky I am, sitting here
watching mountains as if it were a career,

an executive position in a company where
workers who only talk about mountains

get to sort mail in the mailroom, but the ones who
actually look at the mountains—maybe look is

too small a word here—love mountains,
president's chairs are waiting for them.

Last night on my way home I thought I saw Zeus,
but it was only the brewery owner,

who is himself a drunk. Zeus, by the way, was not
the smartest god or even the fastest or strongest;

he was only the leader, by which I mean
he watched mountains, maybe even loved them.

Life coaches

I've never been to a Tony Robbins
revival, but I know how those
participants must feel. Once,
Tony came to me as my ex-wife.
She was inspirational at telling me
how to live my life better, to recognize
what the world wanted me to have,
how to be—here it comes—successful.
Sometimes I could even hear the
Robbins cheerleaders cheering me on:
come on, they said in the background
of this poem, you can do it. All I had
to do was sign up for the program and
my successes would have to follow.

Except when you leave the packed
auditorium and it gets all quiet,
maybe late at night on your front porch,
maybe in a small town, and nobody's
there to cheer you on, even Tony,
who has left for another tour, then you
start to see that when you signed up
it's Tony who is getting successful
and you end up back at your day job,
alone, wondering what the hell
just happened.

The guy who couldn't see color

On some show this old guy cries for joy when he sees color for
the first time. Maybe seeing color is a desire we're born with,
I think, or maybe he already has an expectation of something
really special because he's been preached at his whole life about
how much he's been missing, like the kid who feels all left out because

the other kids got measles and he didn't, not that seeing color
is like getting measles, but maybe seeing only black and white is
something we'd choose, if we could, probably not. But then, what
has color ever done for us?

Nyel might not walk again. He got that black-and-white news
from a green hospital full of multi-colored machines,
not one of which will help him regain his apathetic white leg,
and I wonder if having two legs that work is a desire we're born with,
or is there a way one leg is better?

Poetry sometimes pushes the personal into the vast, revealing
a lesson we can sometimes agree with. Not here. I just want to tell you
about Nyel, how for so many years he loved to work, to run his red
bookstore, to cook colorful meals, to move his two good legs.

I saw a pink skateboarder today on my way to a brown coffee shop.
He was moving down the sidewalk really good,
but he had no legs and a purple shirt and I have no way
to tell you how that has left me.

My life as money

I don't want you to think I only look at life
in terms of money but when I go to work on Monday
I'm a dollar sign, income for somebody else,
how much work can I do in how little time.

I come home and the house measures me
as square footage, the view from the deck
I don't have, how a second bathroom would help
the resale value, fix up the yellow lawn, etc.

When I'm in the store I watch people
watch me to see how much
I'm going to spend, to see
how big their bonuses will be.

Even love is money. Once someone
left me to go away to college to get a career
and there I was, holding hocked dreams
and working to make a square living.

I sit in the coffee shop
with a three-dollar coffee plus tip and wonder if
there's any other way to count a life
but there is no other way.

Mars

There was this show on the massive amount of food
prepared everyday on a luxury ship, thousands
of pounds of shrimp and chicken and unspeakable
numbers of workers trapped on that boat,
racing against the clock to make every meal perfect.
I don't even know if we have words to judge this.

Sometimes I don't feel like I belong here, like I'm
different in the way a shrimp is different
from a chicken, the way they look at
the world with either feathers or from
underneath the ocean and in the end sharing
space on someone's plate is all they have in common.

Sometimes I feel like I'm from another planet,
you know, like I'm lying there on someone else's plate.
Then I walk down the street watching everyone watch
themselves in store windows believing the same thing,
how different they are. And I start thinking, well, maybe
we are all from Mars or maybe we're already on Mars
and we've been here all along.

And if that's true, then maybe we're not so different after all.

The pursuit of happiness

I've been nothing but
potential my whole life,

holding my ticket to be
the next great writer,

too smart for school but
still aimed toward some

brick-walled college
just on potential's fumes.

Here I am now
with all that promise

stinking with the survival
groceries in the pantry,

remnants of
what could have, should have,

leaving me with this old man
shuffle and the knowing.

Water as water

I love rivers more than oceans,
love their borders,
edges curled
around you
like you're the child
who maybe got lost once
but then came home,
the bond
not quite a
blood brother,
(sharing
a past but with
a different father)
and I never liked
water that moved
either way,
in and out
of your life,
a tide that
never makes
up its mind
and leaves you
standing
on some shore
you can't
recognize.

Manifold destiny

Sixty years ago my parents moved out of L.A. to Oregon,
city to wild, leaving the smog they said, and they packed
with them all of the accoutrements of their people, alarm clocks,
metal tools, political songs, and I'm guessing

the new neighbors looked at them suspiciously although
I can only assure you they never meant harm. And they absorbed
the country life fervently, bought pigs, milked cows,
just tried to fit in inside their worn city clothes.

I'm guessing this was also not looked upon favorably by the locals,
by whom I mean all those Californians who had come before them.
Look, I have no answer about whether my parents should
have immigrated into that small, tar-sided shack in the woods,

raised their own first-generation, borderless immigrants
or stayed reclined under the heat of the California sun, but what
I can tell you is they've lived on that mountain for sixty years
and they act like they've been there forever.

Zero in the denominator

Until now I never understood math,
or at least the concept of zero in
the denominator. Teachers tried
to tell me that zero in the denominator
isn't nothing, or something, or anything;
it isn't even zero. They said instead it's a
question that can't be asked or answered,
like what would the world be like if someone
hadn't invented tires, or if you wouldn't
have left me standing so awkwardly on your
front porch so long ago now. Nobody
can answer what would have happened
so I spend my days not asking, and things
come and go and what might have been is not
something or nothing; it's a zero in the
denominator, just a wish whose candle
was never blown out.

A loaf of bread

My daughter asks me
if I can bake a loaf of
bread for the family
who lost a son to
another bullet.
No. But I will march
to that death house and
hold him close,
hold that child so close until
he breathes dreams again,
take a piece of
his childhood and patch up the
life the bullet pushed out.
I will go up there now and move
his lips until he begins
again to speak and sing,
until some future comes
out, words to his girlfriend,
college counselor,
boss or first wife,
a lover, his kids, strangers.
I will go there and fill back up
the empty bag religious people
revere (an empty vessel
is not better), help him rebuild
his place at the table, rekindle
the dead air where he used to sit.
I will pull him back
from that irrevocable
edge until I can convince him
it was just a passing mistake,

just a second to now go retrieve
a single second to now go retrace
to come back into his own
to come back.

Narrow bridge over the Hamma Hamma River

I have this relationship with the truck drivers:
I trust each of them, with my life, and in return
they toe the highway line dutifully, every time.

I have this relationship with the bridge: I anguish over
the rivets clinging to the rusting metal, but it promises
to hold on to me, every time.

I have this relationship with the river: it announces
that some full moon is about to rise over
the eastern hills, far across the bay, and I answer
with the hum of tires on the old night road.

I have this relationship with you: when I
put down the flowers on the counter you will,
hopefully, give up some freeway in favor
of the chair I leave here, for you, every time.

No bad days, just hard days

This is about my great-grandmother,
or if you read deeper maybe it's about
if my father's stories were accurate,
or whether or not

that's important. It might be about
how easy it is to make assumptions
about people or their times, or even
how hard it is to be right about all that.

It's also possible that all I really want is to
tell you about Arkansas, which is probably
a metaphor for simplicity with grace,
but also pain and all the worlds we can't know.

If you can let yourself believe for a second
that my great-grandmother really did say,
"There are no bad days, just hard days,"
housebound on some storied rocking chair on
some remote rented front porch, somewhere

in Arkansas a long time ago,
I think you will be on the right track.

The economics of my last days of high school

The wooden ties on a California railroad
are responsible for keeping the lubricated
gears of the rich spinning between struggling
points on a map. The spikes that hold those ties
make sure that the distance between the rails
is constant so that the trains can travel fast
and far so exploited workers can keep selling
goods to exploited customers.

Just before I graduated, the Burlington Northern
called me to work on its railroad and I said
yes, because the money was good, but can
you wait a week? I have to finish school so
I can get a diploma. And Burlington Northern
asked why and I didn't know the answer so I went
to work for the railroad to further the class wars
of the West. I learned all this from the hallways
of the school I used to go to.

Old woman

We all try to get what we can
out of life. Me, I could make do
if you give me a job that pays
enough to get me a good
restaurant meal once a month,
but no night shift.
I've had enough of that. Some
people would be content
just to have their kid back,
or to not have to fight some
other gang tonight.
Some people would be happy
to just hold on to their lives
for one more day.

There's this old woman I know
who says she will never get
married again, never wants
even a boyfriend around.
She's happy with her life
she says. And I say happy is
a day without being scared
someone is going to hit you—
hard—or not come home, or
come home and act like you're
not there. I say happy is a word
that can cover a lot of ground.

Multiple choice

Sometimes now I cry more
over the news, even knowing we
all have only a certain number
of tears, but other times I can't
bring myself to give one shit when
some hurricane lashes itself
against us or more people go missing
in this week's war, so I plan
to study to be a scientist so
I can reduce the news to one
big number because nobody
gets emotional over numbers,
or maybe a professor so I can
discuss the news in a lecture
and use it in a pop quiz
where the answer, *"D. suffering,"*
is always the right answer.

Crow spreads his wings

This Indian man is instructing us
about the ways of a Native dance,
with illustrations and young people
regaled in their finest beaded clothing
and they sing and pound drums
and the dancers move in ways I have
never seen and the music is notes

I have never heard, like the sound
creek water makes hitting stones under
a distant crow. The man introduces
a new dance and he calls the dancer
by the wrong name and his young
daughter laughs at him just exactly
the way my daughter laughs at me.

A million crows fly over the world
and if we look up we will see a million
silhouettes, each one as different
as Gene Kelly is to these dancers,
but a daughter's laugh, that,
that sting of wrath wrapped inside
the music of a child's delight, I
think that's the same sound
no matter what dance you do,
no matter what creek you hear.

Why I am not the public drunk

In 1939 Grandpa got a job
introducing Arkansas to
California.
He worked for Cal Worthington
for a while, I am told,
selling big used cars under
bigger banners under
blue California skies.

Sometimes he would
send postcards back home
to his only child, telling
him about the endless lights
and skyline and, if you could
read between the lines,
about the long nights and
shattered whiskey glasses
and all the ladies named Irene.

My father's job was to get
some degrees and raise blond kids
who knew how to shake hands
at social frays.
His job was to stay married—
once—to be healthy,
to break the chain.

Sometimes I stare at a glass of
beer on my table and wonder if
I could be a drunk. And sometimes
I wade knee-deep in an ocean
and don't even remember
the name of California.

And maybe that's my job.
Maybe that's my job.

Bird watching

First, learn some names
and watch for the morphological signs
of wings and bodies.
A crow's wings
splay out differently than a raven's,
falcons are built for speed, etc.

Learn that the Latin name for the goshawk
is *Accipiter gentilis*, so when you see one
run down a *Streptopelia decaocto*,
or Eurasian collared dove,
just above your head
on your way out of the house
one morning, you will recognize the players.

In the second phase you will know
the names but you will also become
attached—you will add dimension, so to speak—
so that when the dove's feathers
float down around you like a soft
falling snow, you will feel the talons digging in.

Eventually, your skills will gather into
a third and final level. Here you will
be able to distinguish sounds, even within
a single bird. The dove, for instance,
has at least two calls. The first is rather
brash, as if the dove is calling to you
from a distance, a call,
perhaps, bordering on demanding.
The other is serene, a
peaceful drone, the sound of a small
child sending off to sleep.

When you hear this latter sound as the
goshawk digs in, icing the dove's fate
in a mask of forever, you will not think
about why, why it is the second sound
you now hear,
the peaceful one and not the imploring one,
but instead you will only move through
the detached down feathers,
not thinking about the
dove's eyes that seem to ask something,
or even the goshawk's eyes
as he challenges you to keep
back from his breakfast,
but only that another
exchange in the world has
taken place, one life for
another.

And you open your car
door,
and get in,
and drive.

Acknowledgment of previous publication

"Freak show" .... The American Journal of Poetry
"A nest blew down" .... The American Journal of Poetry
"Reprise" .... Star 82
"199 words for 29 people" .... The Lake
"Two friends in Bend" .... COG
"Circus" .... Blue Moon, Two Thirds North
"What a dream is" .... New World Writing, Flatbush
"Nature/commerce" .... American Journal of Poetry
"And now, the one, the only,
Casey the Brave" .... Pennsylvania Literary Journal
"Car salesman" .... The Closed Eye Open
"One night in a Mexican restaurant with your
small son, talking about death" .... Hare's Paw
"Obituarians dream in happy words" .... 3rd Wednesday
"Home run" .... Prometheus Dreaming
"Cub scout blows it with Catholic school girl" .... Hamline Lit
"What we can't afford
to tell second graders" .... American Journal of Poetry
"Silence" .... Peatsmoke

"The civil war in side me" .... New World Writing
"The half life of moons" .... Concho River Review
"If I were to define religion" .... Kimera
"Why do we say we
find peace when we die?" .... Pennsylvania Literary Journal
"What if your job" .... Willawaw
"Bad luck comes in threes" .... Bath Magg
"At the acupuncturist's" .... Whimperbang
"A handbook for water" .... A handbook for water
"1963" .... COG
"The first" .... BLUEPEPPER
"Almost" .... COG
"And even now, still" .... Timberline Review
'Comanche" .... Apricity
"I do have hope for the world" .... New World Writing
"3:38 a.m." .... Two Hawks Quarterly
"Muzak" .... Avatar Review
"To the next dove that comes around here" .... Cholla Needles
"Working on the night shift" .... North of Oxford
"Beads for Manhattan" .... Neologism
"The Lodge" .... COG
"Words inside a telephone" .... Poydras
"Geography" .... Common Ground Review
"Anatomous" .... K'in
"Love letters from prison" .... Apricity
"Helping a hard luck lady" .... K'in
"Thick as thieves" .... Open Arts Forum
"Time" .... COG
"Oranges" .... Gravel
"Moon vs. streetlight" .... Writing Disorder
"Grief" .... Common Ground Review
"How God catches us cheating" .... Down in the dirt
"Or so it seems to me" .... Wilderness House
"Natural selection poem" .... Down in the Dirt
"Guitar lessons" .... Star 82

"One morning Good Time Steve
sold me drugs" .... Common Ground Review
"President Kennedy" .... Cholla Needles
"Before names of mountains" .... Timberline Review
"Coming to grips with the sound of water" .... Bangalore Review
"At least one beautiful woman" .... Wilderness House
"Freeways are stories with white lines" .... Hamline Lit
"Building a legend out of Legos" .... Blue Moon
"Shooting toy bullets at the real war" .... Riprap
"The trophy case" .... The Pangolin Review
"Taking water away from a river" .... Cholla Needles
"Even Zeus must get tired of the view sometimes" .... RiverSedge
"Life coaches" .... COG
"The guy who couldn't see color" .... COG
"My life as money" .... vox poetica
"Mars" .... Down in the Dirt
"The pursuit of happiness" .... *A nest blew down*
"Water as water" .... Assisi
"Manifold Destiny" .... Down in the Dirt
"Zero in the denominator" .... Gyroscope Review
"A loaf of bread" .... El Portal
"No bad days, just good days" .... Timberline Review
"The economics of my last days of high school" .... Pangolin Review
"Old maid" .... Open Arts Forum
"Multiple choice" .... Poetry Pacific
"Crow spreads his wings" .... Galway Review
"Why I am not the public drunk" .... Rain Magazine
"Bird watching" .... Wild Roof Journal

Title Index

L

M

N

O

P

R

First Line Index

Symbols

A

D

E

F

I

M

www.ingramcontent.com/pod-product-compliance
Lightning Source LLC
LaVergne TN
LVHW030922080826
845145LV00013B/3018

* 9 7 8 1 5 9 4 9 8 1 3 0 2 *